20TH CENTURY *music*
40s & 50s
FROM WAR TO PEACE

Please visit our web site at: www.garethstevens.com
For a free color catalog describing Gareth Stevens Publishing's list of high-quality books
and multimedia programs, call 1-800-542-2595 or fax your request to (414) 332-3567.

Library of Congress Cataloging-in-Publication Data

Hayes, Malcolm.
    40s & 50s: from war to peace / by Malcolm Hayes.
        p. cm. — (20th century music)
    Includes bibliographical references and index.
    Summary: Discusses the influence of people and events worldwide when music served
  as World War II propaganda even as it blossomed into Broadway and Hollywood musicals,
  big bands, and bebop, then evolved into rock and roll.
    ISBN 0-8368-3033-4 (lib. bdg.)
    1. Music—20th century—History and criticism—Juvenile literature. [1. Music—20th
  century—History and criticism.] I. Title: 40s and 50s. II. Title. III. 20th century music.
  ML3928.H36   2002
  780'.9'04—dc21   2001054225

This North American edition first published in 2002 by
Gareth Stevens Publishing
A World Almanac Education Group Company
330 West Olive Street, Suite 100
Milwaukee, WI 53212 USA

Original edition © 2001 by David West Children's Books. First published in Great Britain
in 2001 by Heinemann Library, Halley Court, Jordan Hill, Oxford OX2 8EJ, a division of Reed
Educational and Professional Publishing Limited. This U.S. edition © 2002 by Gareth Stevens, Inc.
Additional end matter © 2002 by Gareth Stevens, Inc.

Designer: Rob Shone
Editor: James Pickering
Picture Research: Carrie Haines

Gareth Stevens Editor: Patricia Lantier

Photo Credits:
Abbreviations: (t) top, (m) middle, (b) bottom, (l) left, (r) right

Glenn A. Baker/Redferns: page 9(tl).
Hulton Getty: cover (br), pages 15(tr), 26(l), 27(br), 28(bl).
William Gottlieb/Library of Congress/Redferns: pages 4(r), 18(mr), 19(bl), 22(l).
Max Jones Files/Redferns: pages 8(bl), 21(tr).
The Kobal Collection: pages 5(tr), 9(br), 10(m), 10-11(t), 11(b), 22-23(t), 27(t).
Lebrecht Collection: pages 4-5(t, b), 5(br), 6(all), 7(r), 10(b), 12(tr, bl), 13(br), 14(m),
   14-15(t), 15(br), 16(both), 17(all), 23(bl, br), 24(both), 25(both).
Andre LeCoz/Lebrecht Collection: page 12(br).
Nigel Luckhurst/Lebrecht Collection: page 14(bl).
Michael Ochs Archive/Redferns: cover (m), pages 3, 7(tl), 18(b), 20(both), 20-21(t), 26(tr),
   29(tr, mr).
David Redfern/Redferns: pages 19(tl, br), 21(ml), 28(tl).
Rex Features: pages 13(tr), 27(ml).
Rodgers & Hammerstein Organisation/Lebrecht Collection: pages 8(t), 11(m).
Royal Academy of Music/Lebrecht Collection: page 23(mr).
S&G Press Agency/Redferns: page 29(tl).
Chuck Stewart/Redferns: 29(bl).
Kurt Weill Foundation/Lebrecht Collection: page 9(tr).

Printed in the United States of America

1 2 3 4 5 6 7 8 9 06 05 04 03 02

20TH CENTURY music
40s & 50s
FROM WAR TO PEACE

Malcolm Hayes

Gareth Stevens Publishing
A WORLD ALMANAC EDUCATION GROUP COMPANY

CONTENTS

The Glenn Miller Army Air Force Band, with Miller himself playing trombone, was sent from America to Britain in 1944. Their big band, jazz sound was a huge success.

Leonard Bernstein was one of the most talented and versatile musicians America has ever produced. He was equally at home conducting, playing the piano, and composing classical works or musicals.

In the new age of bebop, Charlie Parker was a superstar. During his short life, he changed the face of jazz by exploring new limits of technique and invention.

DISASTER TO RECOVERY

The devastation caused by World War II was so appalling that, even today, the world feels its aftereffects. The United States dropped atomic bombs on two Japanese cities, Hiroshima and Nagasaki, introducing the most destructive weapon ever known to humankind. An uneasy peace followed, with constant tension between the two nuclear superpowers, the United States and the Soviet Union, and the nations that supported them.

Classical music mirrored this new, uncertain world in that it seemed to have no common language or set of values anymore. What did the aggressive musical experiments of the European avant-garde have in common with the more conservative style of famous masters such as England's Benjamin Britten and Russia's Dmitri Shostakovich? This troubled peacetime era, however, did make some musical progress. Jazz and rock developed and flourished in both America and Europe, spurred on by the musical symbols of the age — the long-playing record and the electric guitar.

During Hollywood's golden age of screen musicals, Singin' in the Rain *(1952) was dancer Gene Kelly's (1912–1996) most famous movie.*

Shakespeare's play Henry V *was filmed in 1944, with music by English composer William Walton.*

SIR LAURENCE OLIVIER'S
classic British film

henry V

By
WILLIAM SHAKESPEARE

Sir Laurence Olivier
Robert Newton
Renee Asherson
Leo Genn
George Cole
Robert Helpmann
Leslie Banks

Despite wartime difficulties, Olivier's film Henry V *was as spectacular as its musical score.*

6

ARTISTIC RESISTANCE

World War II affected everyone and everything, including peaceful occupations such as composing. It demanded that almost every major composer of the time get involved in the war effort. Composers found different ways to accomplish their involvement.

CATCHING THE MOOD

In a world of aerial bombing, food rationing, and life-and-death struggle, people could at least cheer themselves up by going to the movies. Films with patriotic stories were popular with both audiences and political authorities. In 1944, English actor Laurence Olivier directed and starred in a film of Shakespeare's play *Henry V*, about England's victory at Agincourt in 1415. The film score by William Walton (1902–1983) is one of the finest ever written.

With quiet but determined resistance, composer Francis Poulenc continued to write music in occupied France.

This photograph of Russian composer Dmitri Shostakovich (left), taken during the siege of Leningrad, was almost certainly posed by Soviet authorities.

GLENN MILLER (1904-1944)

In 1944, England was full of American soldiers preparing to invade German-occupied Europe. These soldiers needed entertainment, and the Glenn Miller Army Air Force Band was just the group to provide it. Miller's tunes, such as "In the Mood" and "Moonlight Serenade," were popular with English listeners, too. On December 15, 1944, Miller was on a plane to Paris, when the plane disappeared. It has never been found.

Glenn Miller's plane was probably shot down.

Arturo Toscanini (1867–1957) refused to conduct in Germany or Italy while Hitler and Mussolini were in power.

RUSSIA RESISTS

Russian composer Dmitri Shostakovich (1906–1975) was in the city of Leningrad when it was first besieged by the German army. The heroic resistance depicted in his epic *Leningrad Symphony* (1941) was about Soviet leader Joseph Stalin's savage oppression of his own people, as well the siege itself. At the time, this symphony caught the wartime spirit of nations pulling together. When Arturo Toscanini conducted the western premiere on July 20, 1942, the live radio broadcast in the United States had an audience of twenty million.

PEACEFUL PROTEST

Composers in mainland Europe also found ways to resist German Nazism and Italian Fascism. Luigi Dallapiccola (1904–1975) worked on his masterpiece, the one-act opera *Il Prigioniero,* or *The Prisoner,* (1944–1948) and his idyllic *Greek Lyrics* (1942–1945) while living in hiding in Italy. In German-occupied France, Francis Poulenc (1899–1963) wrote his defiant celebration of liberty, *Figure Humaine,* or *Human Face,* (1943) for unaccompanied chorus. He insisted it should not be performed until after his country was free again.

STAGE MUSICALS

Although, in World War II, American cities were not bombed and shelled the way European cities were, many men and women in the U.S. armed forces were casualties in the Pacific War against the Japanese, and in Europe, too. Musicals helped keep up America's morale.

RODGERS AND HAMMERSTEIN REWRITE THE RULES

Audiences of New York's Broadway theaters liked musicals to be bittersweet stories about city life, such as the world of *Pal Joey* (1940). This musical by composer Richard Rodgers (1902–1979) and lyricist Lorenz Hart (1895–1943) introduced the classic song "Bewitched, Bothered, and Bewildered." The stylized prairie setting of the wildly successful *Oklahoma!* (1943), however, was something new. Composed by Rodgers to lyrics written by Oscar Hammerstein II (1895–1960), *Oklahoma!* also combined song, dance, and drama in a new way. Other immortal Rodgers and Hammerstein musicals included *Carousel* (1945), *South Pacific* (1949), *The King and I* (1951), and *The Sound of Music* (1959).

In 1947, Oklahoma! ran 2,112 performances in New York and 1,458 in London.

Hoagy Carmichael (1899–1981) was in law school when he wrote the classic song "Stardust" (1928). Another one of his hits was "The Nearness of You" (1940).

IRVING BERLIN

More than thirty years after Irving Berlin (1888–1989) became famous with "Alexander's Ragtime Band," his songwriting was still at its peak. *Annie Get Your Gun* (1946) includes such well-known songs as "Anything You Can Do" and "I Got the Sun in the Morning." *Call Me Madam* (1950) was Berlin's last great musical score.

Irving Berlin wrote more than nine hundred songs.

"A MUSICAL PLAY OF MAGNIFICENCE AND GLORY!"
—BROOKS ATKINSON, N. Y. TIMES

STREET SCENE

ADELPHI THEATRE
54th ST. E. of B'WAY
MATS. WED. R. SAI.

In Street Scene, *Weill aimed for a darker kind of seriousness in a show designed for Broadway.*

9

WEILL LEARNS THE AMERICAN WAY

After moving from Germany to America, Kurt Weill (1900–1950) adapted his skills as an opera composer to the new and different world of Broadway. Among his successes were *Lady in the Dark* (1941) and *One Touch of Venus* (1953). Weill explored darker territory in his Broadway "opera" *Street Scene* (1947) and in his last musical, *Lost in the Stars* (1949), which is about apartheid in South Africa.

FROM COLE PORTER TO LERNER AND LOEWE

Cole Porter's songs in Kiss Me, Kate *were composed to his own lyrics.*

Kiss Me, Kate (1948), which was loosely based on Shakespeare's comedy *The Taming of the Shrew,* was graced with a classic score by Cole Porter (1891–1964). The words of Alan Jay Lerner (1918–1986) and the music of German-born Frederick Loewe (1901–1988) immortalized the productions of *Brigadoon* (1947) and *My Fair Lady* (1956).

MOVIE MUSICALS

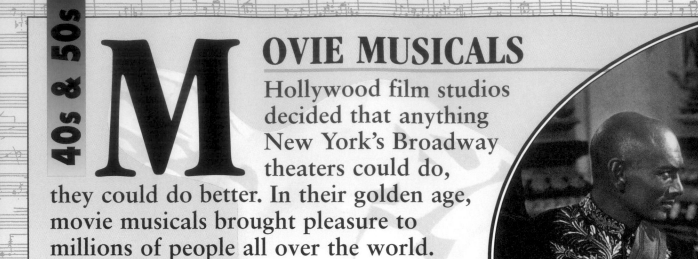

Hollywood film studios decided that anything New York's Broadway theaters could do, they could do better. In their golden age, movie musicals brought pleasure to millions of people all over the world. They still do today.

REVIVING CLASSICS

Show Boat (1927), with its sparkling score by Jerome Kern (1885–1945) and lyrics by Oscar Hammerstein II, had already been filmed in 1929 and 1936, but MGM studios produced a stunning new version in 1951, starring Howard Keel and Ava Gardner. Rodgers and Hart's *Pal Joey* (1940) took on a new life in Columbia's 1957 film, with Frank Sinatra, Rita Hayworth, and Kim Novak.

TWO OF THE BEST

Irving Berlin's *Annie Get Your Gun* (1946), with Howard Keel and Betty Hutton, was released by MGM in 1950. The Broadway hit *Guys and Dolls* (1950), with words and music by Frank Loesser (1910–1969), starred Marlon Brando, Frank Sinatra, and Jean Simmons when it was released on film in 1955.

"There's No Business Like Show Business" and "The Girl That I Marry" are famous songs from Irving Berlin's musical Annie Get Your Gun.

RODGERS AND HAMMERSTEIN'S
SOUTH PACIFIC
IN TODD-AO COLOUR BY TECHNICOLOR
Produced at and Distributed by 20th Century Fox
A SOUTH PACIFIC ENTERPRISES INC. PRODUCTION
STARRING
ROSSANO BRAZZI
MITZI GAYNOR
JOHN KERR
PRODUCED BY
BUDDY ADLER
DIRECTED BY
JOSHUA LOGAN

In 1958, the soundtrack of Rodgers and Hammerstein's musical South Pacific topped album record charts in the United States for thirty-one weeks, and in Britain for 115 weeks.

10

Yul Brynner was the King of Siam in Broadway's 1951 staging of The King and I. *Deborah Kerr joined him in the 1956 film.*

RODGERS AND HAMMERSTEIN

Rodgers and Hammerstein's unusual subject matter and strong characters gave their musicals great depth and scope. As a result, their work transferred remarkably well to the big screen. The spectacular results can be seen in the film versions of *Oklahoma!* (1955), *The King and I* (1956), *South Pacific* (1958), and *The Sound of Music* (1965).

Rodgers (left) *and Hammerstein*

HOLLYWOOD CREATIONS

Some of America's best musicals were created for the big screen from the start. Bing Crosby had a huge hit with the Irving Berlin song "White Christmas" in Paramount studio's *Holiday Inn* (1942), but many of the greatest musical successes came from MGM. Gene Kelly starred with Fred Astaire and Judy Garland in *Easter Parade* (1948), also with songs by Berlin, and with Leslie Caron in *An American in Paris* (1951), with music by George Gershwin and screenplay by Alan Jay Lerner. Kelly's greatest triumph, however, was *Singin' in the Rain* (1952) with Debbie Reynolds. MGM's charming *Gigi* (1958), with songs by Lerner and Loewe, starred Leslie Caron and Maurice Chevalier.

Set in the 1920s, when silent movies were being replaced by "talkies," Singin' in the Rain cleverly blended its story line with Arthur Freed's and Nacio Herb Brown's songs.

11

NEW BEGINNINGS

America offered a haven to many European composers fleeing from Nazism and the war. These new arrivals enriched the music of America with their own, deep-rooted classical traditions. Other European composers continued to work at home.

RELUCTANT EXILES

Austria's Arnold Schoenberg (1874–1951) settled in Los Angeles, where he composed some late masterpieces, including his String Trio (1945) and *A Survivor from Warsaw* (1947), which focuses on an eyewitness account of Nazi ferocity toward Jews in the Warsaw ghetto. Hungary's Béla Bartók (1881–1945) found life in New York difficult, but he still wrote his highly successful Concerto for Orchestra (1943) and Third Piano Concerto (1945). Germany's Paul Hindemith (1895–1963) composed while teaching at Yale University, before he moved to Switzerland in 1953.

ONLY RECITAL THIS SEASON

Szigeti

Assisted by *ENDRE PETRI* at the Piano

Guest Artist
BENNY GOODMAN

Monday Evening
JANUARY 9
at 8:30 o'clock

PROGRAM OVERLEAF

First Performance Anywhere of
BELA BARTÓK'S RHAPSODY
FOR CLARINET, VIOLIN and PIANO
(Written for Benny Goodman and Joseph Szigeti)

CARNEGIE HALL

American jazz clarinetist Benny Goodman impressed Hungarian composer Béla Bartók, who wrote the chamber piece Contrasts *(1938) for him. Goodman and violinist Josef Szigeti performed at Carnegie Hall, with Bartók at the piano.*

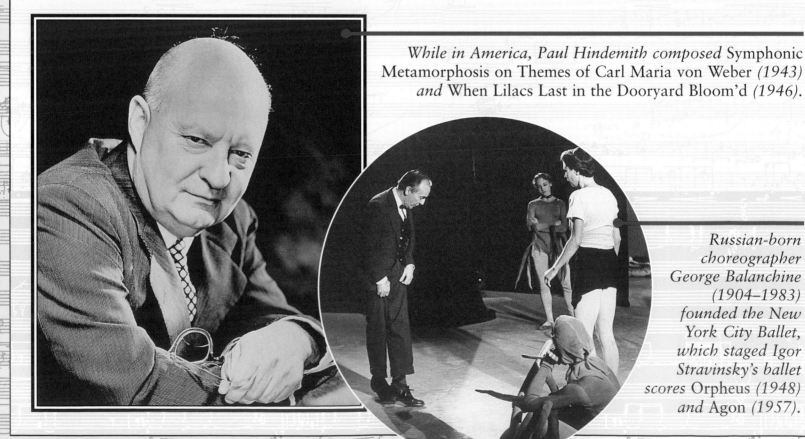

While in America, Paul Hindemith composed Symphonic Metamorphosis on Themes of Carl Maria von Weber *(1943) and* When Lilacs Last in the Dooryard Bloom'd *(1946).*

Russian-born choreographer George Balanchine (1904–1983) founded the New York City Ballet, which staged Igor Stravinsky's ballet scores Orpheus *(1948) and* Agon *(1957).*

AN ENGLISH SYMPHONIST

In wartime, England's Ralph Vaughan Williams (1872–1958) produced his serene Fifth Symphony (1943). In peacetime, still full of surprises in his old age, Vaughan Williams wrote his much bleaker Sixth Symphony (1947). Three more symphonies followed. In 1951, Vaughan Williams completed his masterpiece, the opera *The Pilgrim's Progress*, which was based on a 16th-century story written by John Bunyan.

STAYING PUT

Richard Strauss's (1864–1949) status as Germany's senior composer meant he could live out the war at home without too much difficulty. His grief-laden *Metamorphosen*, or *Transformations*, (1945) for string orchestra was his response to the destruction of Germany's opera houses by British and American bombing. Strauss's *Four Last Songs* (1948) were another late masterpiece. Austria's Anton von Webern (1883–1945) stayed at home through the war, too, composing his two Cantatas (1940 and 1943). In 1945, Webern was accidentally killed by an American soldier.

ART MUST GO ON

Igor Stravinsky (1882–1971) was born in Russia but lived for many years in France. With his move to America in 1940, Stravinsky had been exiled twice from his homeland. In spite of all this moving around, he wrote a dazzling sequence of major works, ranging from his opera *The Rake's Progress* (1951), which is still staged regularly today, to the ultra-concentrated *Requiem Canticles* (1966), the serial technique of which was influenced by the works of Schoenberg and Webern.

Stravinsky eventually became an American citizen.

Webern composed his last and greatest works isolated in Austria, where the Nazis had banned his music.

OPERA REBORN

When peace arrived in 1945, opera, the most complicated and expensive medium of classical music, was once again a realistic option. The rebirth of interest in opera was particularly encouraged by the achievements of one brilliant English composer.

THE DAWN OF POST-WAR OPERA

A committed pacifist, composer Benjamin Britten (1913–1976) left England in 1939 to live in the United States, which was then a neutral country. In 1942, he returned to England and began work on his opera *Peter Grimes*. The story is about a Suffolk fisherman who is a misfit in his own community and whose life is destroyed by intolerance and misfortune. *Peter Grimes* premiered in 1945. Its great success not only made Britten famous but also single-handedly set in motion the post-war tradition of modern opera.

Britten (left) accompanies Pears in a song recital.

Britten (right) and librettist Robert Duncan (b. 1919), an American poet, review the score of The Rape of Lucretia *in the garden at Glyndebourne Festival Opera.*

Britten's opera The Turn of the Screw *is based on a ghost story by American writer Henry James (1843–1916).*

14

BRITTEN AND PEARS

Besides *Peter Grimes* and many works for the concert hall, Britten wrote two large-scale operas, *Billy Budd* (1951) and *Gloriana* (1953), and several operas for smaller groups, including *The Rape of Lucretia* (1946), *Albert Herring* (1947), *The Little Sweep* (1949) and *The Turn of the Screw* (1954). Most of the leading roles were written for Britten's partner, tenor Peter Pears.

Tippett watches a rehearsal of his oratorio A Child of Our Time *(1941), inspired by a young Czech's protest against Nazism.*

OTHER COMPOSERS JOIN IN

In 1952, two English composers responded to the challenge of *Peter Grimes* in their own different ways. Michael Tippett (1905–1998) followed Britten's opera with *The Midsummer Marriage*, and William Walton, who was living in Italy at the time, completed *Troilus and Cressida*, which was set during the Trojan War in Ancient Greece. In France, Francis Poulenc wrote an unusual masterpiece. His *Dialogues des Carmélites* (1957) is about the fate of a community of Carmelite nuns during the French Revolution.

Hans Werner Henze's originality quickly established him as a leading composer in the post-war music world.

HENZE REVIVES GERMAN OPERA

Germany's two hundred opera houses needed a productive new composer, and Hans Werner Henze (*b.* 1926) met the demand. First came *Boulevard Solitude* (1952), an updated version of the *Manon Lescaut* story used many years earlier by Italy's Giacomo Puccini. Henze's strange and colorful fairy-tale opera, *König Hirsch*, or *King Stag*, (1956), was followed by the historical drama *Der Prinz von Homburg*, or *The Prince of Homburg*, (1960).

RUSSIA AND EASTERN EUROPE

During World War II and afterward, Joseph Stalin and the Soviet Communist Party terrorized the lives of millions of people. Even Stalin's death in 1953 did not bring much relief. Composers still had to follow the dictates of the Soviet state.

PROKOFIEV'S *CINDERELLA*

Sergei Prokofiev's (1891–1953) opera *War and Peace* (1943), based on Leo Tolstoy's novel about Napoleon's 1812 invasion of Russia, caught Russia's patriotic wartime mood. So did his Fifth Symphony (1945). His ballet *Cinderella* (1945) was also successful, but his much darker Sixth Symphony (1947) was officially disliked. Prokofiev died on March 5, 1953 — ironically, the same day as Stalin.

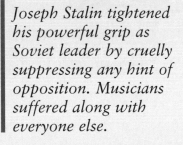

Joseph Stalin tightened his powerful grip as Soviet leader by cruelly suppressing any hint of opposition. Musicians suffered along with everyone else.

"DO AS YOU'RE TOLD"

The Soviet Union's big idea for classical music was that it should be about "Socialist realism." Operas and ballets about the heroic deeds of Russian workers and peasants were acceptable, but anything Soviet authorities disliked was denounced as "modernist" or "formalist." In 1948, Tikhon Khrennikov (b. 1913) became head of the Soviet Composers' Union and began an official crackdown. Dmitri Shostakovich and Sergei Prokofiev both were denounced.

Khrennikov (left) composed many works that conformed to the doctrine of "Socialist realism." He is pictured here at a rehearsal with Boris Khaikin (1904–1978), the conductor of Moscow's Bolshoi Opera.

16

The story of Cinderella has inspired many classical composers.

Along with Spartacus, Gayaneh (1942) was Khachaturian's other full-length ballet. It contains the immensely entertaining "Sabre Dance," which has become popular around the world.

David Oistrakh (1908–1974) was one of the great violinists of the century. He was the first to perform Khachaturian's Violin Concerto. Shostakovich dedicated his two concertos to Oistrakh.

A VOICE FROM ARMENIA

Aram Khachaturian (1903–1978) was one of the few Soviet composers who successfully balanced individual talent with the restrictions of official demands. His Violin Concerto (1940) drew brilliantly on the folk music of his Armenian heritage. His colorful, passionately tuneful ballet *Spartacus* (1954), about a slave who led a rebellion against Ancient Rome, was a safe, "revolutionary" subject and was highly regarded.

SHOSTAKOVICH PERSISTS — AND SURVIVES

Dmitri Shostakovich was too internationally famous and successful to be silenced or sent to a labor camp, as millions of other Russians were. Even so, until Stalin's death, he wrote very little outside of patriotic cantatas and chamber or piano music. Shostakovich's Tenth Symphony (1953) brought him back into official Soviet favor. In 1955, he reworked his First Violin Concerto (1948), and in 1957, he composed his Eleventh Symphony, subtitled *The Year 1905*. Next came his First Cello Concerto (1959), and between 1944 and 1960, he wrote the Second to Eighth of his fifteen String Quartets.

BIG BAND TO BEBOP

Bebop was the cutting edge of jazz in the 1940s. Despite having very different roots, it mirrored some aspects of modernism in classical music. Bebop explored extremes of harmony, just as classical "atonality" had done forty years earlier, and gifted soloists dominated this type of jazz.

Thelonius Monk (1917–1982) studied briefly at New York's classical Juilliard School. By the 1940s, he was playing in clubs with Dizzy Gillespie and saxophonist Coleman Hawkins (1904–1969). His music was so advanced it confused many listeners.

MASTER OF A NEW STYLE

Miles Davis (1926–1991) was trained in classical music. He studied trumpet at the Juilliard School of Music in New York but soon moved toward jazz, playing with Charlie Parker (1920–1955) and Dizzy Gillespie (1917–1993). As the wartime popularity of traditional big bands began to wane, bebop caught on. Davis's understated mastery on trumpet and flugelhorn, and his "cool" style, became an alternative to Dizzy Gillespie's over-the-top flamboyance.

Miles Davis fronted a band in the 1950s. His album Kind of Blue *(1959) is often considered the greatest jazz record of all time.*

CHARLIE PARKER

Known as "Yardbird" or "Bird," Charlie Parker was bebop's genius. At various stages of his career, Parker worked with Gillespie, Davis, and Monk. Parker's composing and saxophone playing, mostly on an alto instrument rather than on the more usual tenor sax, set new standards of rhythmic and melodic invention. Today, Charlie "Yardbird" Parker is still regarded as one of jazz's greatest soloists.

18

BEBOP'S FATHER FIGURE

Even before the 1940s bebop "boom," Dizzy Gillespie and his trumpet were featured stars in several big bands, including one led by pianist Earl Hines (1903–1983). Gillespie specialized in fantastic flights of virtuosity on a trumpet with its bell pointing upward at an angle. Once while trying out an instrument that accidentally had been bent, he found that his ear could pick up the notes more quickly. Gillespie was a strong supporter of rising younger talent and collaborated with trumpeters Miles Davis and Clifford Brown (1930–1956).

"TRANE" SOUNDS

John Coltrane (1926–1967) made his name playing, first, with Dizzy Gillespie, then, with Miles Davis. Although he usually played tenor saxophone, he sometimes played soprano sax or the flute, too. "Trane," as his fans christened him, developed a style that blended great virtuosity with a tougher, rasping tone that became known as "hard bop." In 1957, he played in a quartet with pianist Thelonius Monk at New York's popular Five Spot Cafe.

In the mid-1940s, bebop made its real breakthrough with Dizzy Gillespie's quintet, which included Charlie Parker. Early audiences were bewildered by this new sound.

Parker was given the nickname "Bird" because he loved fried chicken!

Coltrane started out on alto sax but made his name playing the larger and deeper-toned tenor instrument. The sounds he produced were unlike anything heard before.

19

ELLINGTON AND OTHERS

In jazz, as in classical music, the greatest artists have a way of flourishing even after their music is "out of style." Duke Ellington (1899–1974) survived the decline of the big band era of the early 1940s in great style.

SYMPHONIC JAZZ

Working with composer-arranger Billy Strayhorn (1915–1967), Duke Ellington expanded jazz forms in a symphonic way, sometimes using a classical orchestra. In January 1943, his 48-minute *Black, Brown and Beige* was played at New York's Carnegie Hall. In the early 1950s, however, even Ellington's immense talents as a pianist, composer, arranger, and big band leader could not stop his popularity from fading into the shadow of bebop. This tide suddenly turned one legendary night at the 1956 Newport Jazz Festival, where his band's late-night session was a sensational success. For the rest of his life, Ellington triumphantly toured the world.

Lester Young's mastery of the saxophone was so remarkable that Billie Holiday nicknamed him "The President."

GRAPPELLI AND REINHARDT

French violinist Stéphane Grappelli (1908–1997) and Belgian guitarist Django Reinhardt (1910–1953) founded the Quintette du Hot Club de France. By the 1940s, its elegantly roguish style had become world-famous. Then, Grappelli and Reinhardt went their separate ways. After World War II, Reinhardt played briefly with Ellington in the United States before reforming the Quintette, reappearing at times with Grappelli.

Reinhardt (seated, second from left) and Grappelli (right) with the Quintette

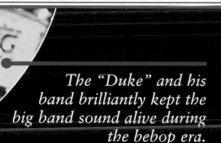

The "Duke" and his band brilliantly kept the big band sound alive during the bebop era.

Virtuoso bassist Charles Mingus first collaborated with Charlie Parker, Miles Davis, Duke Ellington, and others. Then he led a series of "Jazz Workshop" bands, working with many different artists.

One of the world's greatest blues singers, Billie Holiday gave a legendary concert at Carnegie Hall in 1948.

BASS PLAYING TAKES OFF

Charles Mingus (1922–1979) was one of jazz's great bass players. The traditional function of a bass was to provide harmonic support to the other instruments, but Mingus's playing could also imitate the freedom of saxophone, piano, and trumpet melodies. Also a composer, Mingus applied Ellington's idea of working with expanded forms to smaller groups. His "Open Letter to Duke" from *Mingus Ah Um* (1959) is his tribute to the great man.

TENOR SAX STYLES

Coleman Hawkins and Lester Young (1909–1959) were not composers, but their contrasting styles of saxophone playing had a big impact on the music world. Hawkins had a sharp, weighty sound that transferred well from big band to bebop. Young's playing was gentler and more reflective, and worked beautifully with the poignant blues voice of Billie Holiday (1915–1959). Ben Webster (1909–1973) moved easily between rasping virtuosity and smooth lyricism.

BERNSTEIN AND COPLAND

Leonard Bernstein (1918–1990) had a powerful influence on American music. He excelled as a composer of classical music, jazz, and musicals. He was also a gifted pianist and one of the finest conductors of his time.

When Leonard Bernstein was studying piano at Harvard, Aaron Copland encouraged him to compose his First Symphony (1942). Subtitled Jeremiah, it was the first of Bernstein's several classical works on Jewish subjects. Soon afterward came the musical On the Town (1944).

THE ALL-AROUND STAR

As a classical conductor, in 1943, Bernstein replaced a sick colleague with only a few hours' notice and became famous overnight. He also achieved success quickly in his composing. *The Age of Anxiety* (1949), which is the subtitle of Bernstein's Second Symphony, includes a brilliant piano part that Bernstein played himself at the premiere. He also wrote ballet scores, including *Fancy Free* (1944), a violin Serenade (1954), and the one-act opera *Trouble in Tahiti* (1952).

A MASTER OF MUSICALS

Jazz was a natural part of Bernstein's style, especially the bold, brassy sound of the big bands. His *Prelude, Fugue, and Riffs* (1949) exists in separate versions for orchestra and jazz band. Jazz also colors Bernstein's musicals — *On the Town* (1944, filmed in 1949), *Wonderful Town* (1953, filmed in 1955 as *My Sister Eileen*), *Candide* (1956), and the fabulously successful *West Side Story* (1957, filmed in 1961).

BERNSTEIN'S
ON THE WATERFRONT

A grim story of life on the docks and labor union corruption, Elia Kazan's *On the Waterfront* (1954) is one of the great films of the 1950s. It starred Marlon Brando (*b*. 1924), was showered with Oscars, and featured Bernstein's only film score, which was remarkable for its driving energy and strong atmosphere.

Although Bernstein did not receive an Academy Award for On the Waterfront, *Brando* (right) *won the Best Actor Oscar.*

Besides Copland's popular ballet scores, his many works include a Clarinet Concerto (1948) written for Benny Goodman and Twelve Poems of Emily Dickinson *(1950).*

MUSIC FOR THE PEOPLE

Aaron Copland (1900–1990) believed classical music needed popular appeal as well as high seriousness. His *Fanfare for the Common Man* (1942) became the basis of his Third Symphony (1946). While his opera *The Tender Land* (1952) has never had the success it deserves, his ballets *Rodeo* (1942) and *Appalachian Spring* (1944) were worldwide hits. Copland's Piano Quartet (1950) employs aspects of Schoenberg's serial technique, but with different results.

Copland's ballet Appalachian Spring *was set in a pioneer community in Pennsylvania. The story centers around a young, newly married couple setting up a home together.*

The original choreography for Appalachian Spring *was by Martha Graham. She became known as the high priestess of modern dance, which she developed far beyond classical ballet.*

MARTHA GRAHAM
AND HER
DANCE GROUP

MESSIAEN AND THE AVANT-GARDE

Surrounded by cities that had been destroyed by bombing, many of the younger generation of European composers were determined that modern music would break away from a world that had brought about so much devastation. For this generation, the mood of the time was "New Music Starts Here."

SURVIVE AND PROSPER

Olivier Messiaen (1908–1992) received his musical education at the Paris Conservatoire. In 1940, while serving in the French armed forces, he was captured by the German army and imprisoned at a camp in Poland. There he composed his *Quartet for the End of Time* (1941) and played the piano in the first performance of this work for an audience of five thousand fellow prisoners. Messiaen was released in 1941 and returned to France, where he became a professor at the Conservatoire. Some brilliant works followed, among them the spectacular, ten-movement *Turangalîla-symphonie* (1948).

One of Messiaen's pupils was Jean Barraqué (1928–1973), who combined avant-garde technique with the classical style of Beethoven. Barraqué's small but remarkable output included a Séquence (1950–1955) for soprano and instruments.

Messiaen's classes at the Paris Conservatoire attracted many talented young musicians. One of them was the brilliant pianist Yvonne Loriod (b. 1924), who became Messiaen's second wife.

Boulez (left) *and Stockhausen* (right) *with Maderna in the 1950s*

THE YOUNG LIONS

Messiaen taught several of the leading young composers of the day, including France's Pierre Boulez (*b.* 1925) and Germany's Karlheinz Stockhausen (*b.* 1928). Boulez's chamber work *Le Marteau sans Maître* (1954) is a brilliant modern classic. Stockhausen worked on a larger scale in his ultra-complex *Gruppen*, or *Groups*, (1955–57) for three orchestras. He also experimented with electronic sounds on tape in *Gesang der Jünglinge*, or *Song of the Youths*, (1956). In Italy, Luigi Nono (1924–1990) composed his choral work *Il Canto Sospeso*, or *The Suspended Song*, (1956), using the words of resistance fighters who had been executed in the war.

AMERICAN RADICALS

Most American composers were less interested in following the radical path explored before the war by Schoenberg and Webern. An exception, however, was Elliott Carter (*b.* 1908), who developed an expansive style of modernism in his First and Second String Quartets (1951 and 1959). After a long creative silence, French-born Edgar Varèse (1883–1965), who became an American citizen, produced both *Déserts* (1954) and *Poème Eléctronique* (1958) using electronic tape.

Like his country's opera composers, Italian Luigi Nono wrote brilliantly for voices. His political stance inspired his choral work Epitaffio per Federico García Lorca *(1953), a memorial to the poet, Lorca, who was killed in the Spanish Civil War in 1936.*

25

STAR PERFORMERS

The rise of popular media, especially radio, television, films, and vinyl long-playing records (LPs), meant that the musical stars of the new age made songwriters and composers famous, rather than the other way around.

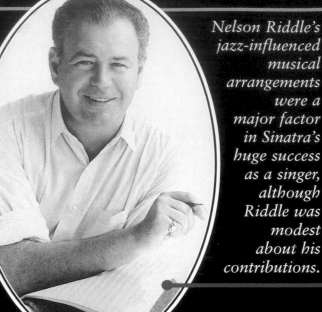

Nelson Riddle's jazz-influenced musical arrangements were a major factor in Sinatra's huge success as a singer, although Riddle was modest about his contributions.

A TRULY GREAT ENTERTAINER

Frank Sinatra (1915–1998) started making a name for himself while singing with the Dorsey Brothers' band in the early 1940s. Within a few years, he was a huge star as a soloist and film actor. His successes in musicals included Leonard Bernstein's *On the Town* (1949) and Frank Loesser's *Guys and Dolls* (1955). *Songs for Swingin' Lovers* (1956), with its careful arrangements by Nelson Riddle (1921–1985), is one of Sinatra's many classic recordings. With his unique style and ability to time a phrase, Sinatra's appeal easily outlasted changes in musical fashion.

The four-beats-to-a-bar style of swing, with its blend of easy charm and sharp rhythm, was Sinatra's natural territory. Working with Nelson Riddle and other arrangers, he recorded a sequence of legendary albums that included Songs for Young Lovers, This is Sinatra, A Swingin' Affair, Come Fly With Me, *and* Swing Easy!

Much of the popularity of Ella Fitzgerald's Songbook *LPs was due to producer Norman Granz, who signed her to his Verve record label. Fitzgerald also recorded three albums with Louis Armstrong.*

Bing Crosby (left), Dorothy Lamour, and Bob Hope in the film The Road to Bali (1952)

BING CROSBY

Bing Crosby (1903–1977) started out as a talented jazz singer, working with bandleaders such as Paul Whiteman (1890–1967) and Duke Ellington, among others. Movie-goers saw a different Bing Crosby — the likable crooner who starred in *Holiday Inn* (1942) and *Blue Skies* (1946), both featuring songs by Irving Berlin. *High Society* (1956), with songs by Cole Porter, was Crosby's only film appearance with Frank Sinatra.

AN IMMORTAL SINGER

The artistry of Ella Fitzgerald (1917–1996) was on the same level as Sinatra's, but she was closer to being a true jazz singer and had a brilliant flair for "scat." From the early 1940s, she was the undisputed "First Lady" of American popular song. In her *Songbook* series of recordings, Fitzgerald performs songs written by Gershwin, Berlin, Kern, Porter, and Ellington in a way that will probably never be surpassed.

Louis Armstrong's success as a singer proved that, in jazz, style can count for much more than true vocal quality. He appeared on stage with Velma Middleton in 1956.

ARMSTRONG CONQUERS THE WORLD

Louis Armstrong (1900–1971) grew up in New Orleans, the original home of jazz. He was known around the world as "Satchmo," the gravel-voiced singer and entertainer whom many consider the finest jazz trumpeter ever. His "scat" singing was also among the best. Armstrong's traditional style of trumpet playing was formed before the bebop era, but his popularity always remained strong.

ROCK 'N' ROLL

No one today seriously argues about when rock 'n' roll truly began. In 1956, Elvis Presley (1935–1977) recorded "Heartbreak Hotel." No single recording in history has ever had a bigger impact.

Bill Haley (center) and the Comets paved the way for Presley's success with their classic "Rock Around the Clock" (1955).

28

THE LEGEND BEGINS

Presley's gift was blending a smoldering delivery with an instinctive appeal to the rebellious attitudes of millions of teenagers. His tough-minded manager, Colonel Tom Parker, kept the hits rolling out, among them, "Hound Dog, " "Blue Suede Shoes," and "Don't Be Cruel." Next came Elvis's screen musicals, including *Love Me Tender, Loving You, Jailhouse Rock,* and *King Creole,* with title songs to match. Two years of U.S. Army service in Germany followed. Now Elvis had a clean-cut image and a singing style that was closer to crooning. Critics accused him of becoming lazy with success, but his fans never stopped loving him.

A SHORT BUT SWEET CAREER

The "King" came home from army service without his sideburns, but he had just as much superstar appeal as before.

Like Elvis Presley, Buddy Holly (1936–1959) drew together different influences, such as rhythm and blues and teenage pop, to form his own style of rock 'n' roll. With his group, The Crickets, he developed a fresh, breezy songwriting style. Some of Holly's best numbers, such as "That'll Be the Day" and "Peggy Sue" (both 1957), were huge hits before he died in an airplane crash.

Holly (center) was one of the first big stars to use the popular Fender Stratocaster guitar.

SINGING TOGETHER

Don and Phil Everly (*b.* 1937 and 1939) started out with a pleasant, close-harmony duet style that was popular in the American South. Elvis Presley's impact suddenly made this sound seem too tame. The brothers responded with "Bye Bye Love" (1957), which had a stronger rock 'n' roll beat and quickly sold a million records.

CHUCK BERRY

Rock developed in America by blending several musical styles, one of which was rhythm and blues. This style had been developed from its blues ancestry by Howlin' Wolf (1910–1976), Muddy Waters (1915–1983), and Little Richard (*b.* 1931). Chuck Berry (*b.* 1926), however, with his singer-songwriting talent and thunderous electric guitar, was the biggest influence on generations of rockers to come.

Berry's flamboyance on stage was a real crowd-pleaser.

29

Little Richard pioneered rock 'n' roll's trademark lyric "awop-bopaloo-bop-awop-bam-boom!"

Don and Phil Everly became major stars with hits like "Wake Up, Little Susie" and "All I Have to Do Is Dream" (both 1957).

· TIME LINE ·

	WORLD EVENTS	MUSICAL EVENTS	THE ARTS	FAMOUS MUSICIANS	MUSICAL WORKS
1940	• World War II: Hitler conquers France	• Copland's Billy the Kid first performed	• First Bugs Bunny cartoon	• Beatles John Lennon and Ringo Starr born	• Britten: Sinfonia da Requiem for orchestra
1941	• Japanese attack Pearl Harbor; U.S. enters war	• Weill's musical Lady in the Dark staged	• Bogart stars in The Maltese Falcon	• American singer Bob Dylan born	• Duke Ellington: "Take the A Train"
1942	• Battle of Midway: Japan's first major defeat	• Copland's ballet Rodeo staged	• Bergman and Bogart star in Casablanca	• Death of composer Alexander von Zemlinsky	• Prokofiev: Seventh Piano Sonata
1943	• Fall of Mussolini in Italy	• Broadway premiere of musical Oklahoma!	• Children's story The Little Prince published	• Mick Jagger and Keith Richards born	• Vaughan Williams: Fifth Symphony
1944	• Allies land in France and drive back Germans	• Dizzy Gillespie joins Billy Eckstine's band	• Somerset Maugham: The Razor's Edge	• Glenn Miller dies in plane crash	• Copland and Graham: Appalachian Spring
1945	• Germany and Japan surrender; war ends	• Premiere of Britten's opera Peter Grimes	• George Orwell: Animal Farm	• Deaths of Bela Bartók and Anton von Webern	• Rodgers and Hammerstein: Carousel
1946	• UN General Assembly holds first meetings	• Film release of musical Annie Get Your Gun	• Film release of It's a Wonderful Life	• Tenor vocalist José Carreras born	• Britten: The Rape of Lucretia
1947	• India and Pakistan gain independence	• Thelonious Monk forms his first band	• Cannes Film Festival opens • Camus: The Plague	• Rock artist David Bowie born	• Schoenberg: A Survivor from Warsaw
1948	• South Africa: apartheid begins	• Premiere of Cole Porter's Kiss Me, Kate	• Film release of Key Largo	• Violinist Pinchas Zukerman born	• Messiaen: Turangalîla-symphonie
1949	• NATO formed • People's Republic of China formed	• Broadway musical South Pacific staged	• Arthur Miller: Death of a Salesman	• Death of composer Richard Strauss	• Weill: Lost in the Stars
1950	• Korean War begins • China invades Tibet	• Broadway musical Guys and Dolls staged	• Kurosawa directs Rashomon	• American soul musician Stevie Wonder born	• Malcolm Arnold: first set of English Dances
1951	• Libya becomes an independent country	• Broadway musical The King and I staged	• Television show I Love Lucy first broadcast	• Death of pianist Artur Schnabel	• Britten: Billy Budd
1952	• America tests the first hydrogen bombs	• Film release of Singin' in the Rain	• Film release of From Here to Eternity	• New Wave musician David Byrne born	• Tippett: The Midsummer Marriage
1953	• USSR: Death of Stalin; Khrushchev in power	• Premiere of Shostakovich's Tenth Symphony	• Arthur Miller: The Crucible	• Death of English composer Arnold Bax	• Kurt Weill: One Touch of Venus
1954	• U.S. launches first nuclear submarine	• Premiere of Walton's Troilus and Cressida	• William Golding: Lord of the Flies	• American singer Rickie Lee Jones born	• Boulez: Le Marteau sans Maître
1955	• Warsaw Pact formed • South Africa leaves UN	• Film release of Oklahoma!	• James Dean stars in East of Eden	• Death of American jazz musician Charlie Parker	• Igor Stravinsky: Canticum Sacrum
1956	• Uprisings in Hungary and Poland	• Elvis Presley records "Heartbreak Hotel"	• Beckett: Waiting for Godot	• Death of American jazz pianist Art Tatum	• Messiaen: Oiseaux Exotiques
1957	• European Common Market (EEC) founded	• Premiere of Boulez's Third Piano Sonata	• Film release of Bridge on the River Kwai	• Death of Jean Sibelius	• Leonard Bernstein: West Side Story
1958	• CND starts antibomb protests	• Start of the British LP chart	• Chevalier and Caron star in Gigi	• American rock artist Michael Jackson born	• Luigi Nono: Cori di Didone
1959	• Cuba: Castro in power • U.S. troops sent to Laos	• Ronnie Scott's jazz club opens in London	• Billy Wilder: Some Like It Hot	• Buddy Holly dies in plane crash	• Elliott Carter: Second String Quartet

GLOSSARY

avant-garde: members of an artistic movement that is more challenging or experimental than conventional or traditional artistic styles.

big band: a large orchestra or group of musicians, usually associated with jazz or swing, that features ensemble playing as well as solo performances.

blues: a style of music with a melancholy or mournful spirit, which emerged in the deep South and is part of the ancestry of jazz and rock.

cantata: a musical work composed for a chorus accompanied by instruments.

chamber music: instrumental music written for a small group of musicians, intended to be performed in a room or a small concert hall.

flugelhorn: a brass instrument with the sound of a bugle, but looks like and has the keys of a trumpet or a cornet.

librettist: a writer who composes the text for a musical work, such as an opera.

opera: a musical drama that includes vocal pieces accompanied by an orchestra, as well as orchestral overtures and interludes.

rhythm and blues: a style of popular music that originated in the 1950s and mixes features of blues music with a strong beat and lively rhythms.

scat: a vocal technique of jazz singing that uses a stream of nonsense syllables to imitate the sounds of instruments.

score: the body of music composed for a film or live theater production.

tenor: the highest adult male singing voice; also, refers to a type of saxophone with a particular tone.

virtuoso: a highly skilled musical performer.

MORE BOOKS TO READ

All Shook Up: The Life and Death of Elvis Presley. Barry Denenberg (Scholastic)

American Jazz Musicians. Collective Biographies (series). Stanley I. Mour (Enslow)

Duke Ellington: Jazz Master. Giants of Art and Culture (series). Gene Brown (Blackbirch)

Great African Americans in Jazz. Outstanding African Americans (series). Carlotta Hacker (Crabtree Publishing)

Leonard Bernstein: Composer and Conductor. Jean F. Blashfield (Ferguson Publishing)

The Life and Times of Frank Sinatra. Esme Hawes (Chelsea House)

Louis Armstrong: King of Jazz. African-American Biographies (series). Wendie C. Old (Enslow)

Miles Davis. Impact Biography (series). George R. Crisp (Franklin Watts)

Overture and Finale: Rodgers & Hammerstein and the Creation of Their Two Greatest Hits. Max Wilk (Back Stage Books)

Shake, Rattle, and Roll: The Founders of Rock & Roll. Holly George-Warren (Houghton-Mifflin)

WEB SITES

The History of Jazz Music. *www.jazzhistory.f2s.com*

The Louis Armstrong Tribute Site. *tinpan.fortunecity.com/riff/11/*

More from Billy Strayhorn. *ddmi.he.net/~godfrey/horn/more.htm*

Pop Music: The 50s. *www.yesterdayland.com/ popopedia/shows/decades/music_1950s.php*

Due to the dynamic nature of the Internet, some web sites stay current longer than others. To find additional web sites, use a reliable search engine with one or more of the following keywords: *bebop, big band, Leonard Bernstein, Miles Davis, Bill Haley, Buddy Holly, jazz, Glenn Miller, musicals, Elvis Presley, rock 'n' roll,* and *Frank Sinatra.*

INDEX